PADDLE
PILGRIM

AN ADVENTURE OF LEARNING AND SPIRIT,
KAYAKING THE MISSISSIPPI RIVER

DR. DAVID ELLINGSON

ISBN-10: 1492108960
ISBN-13: 9781492108962

TABLE OF CONTENTS

INTRODUCTION

Why?

The looks on people's faces said it all. For some it was a look of disbelief. For others it shouted, "You are crazy!" For a few it suggested amazement and maybe even admiration. But behind all the expressions was the question, "Why would someone paddle the entire Mississippi River?"

"Why?" Adventure, Learn and Pilgrimage.

Adventure: As a boy I read a wonderful book by Holling C. Holling, *Minn of the Mississippi*, which told the story of a Turtle born near the river headwaters, who over a number of years traveled the entire length of the Mississippi. In beautiful pictures and stirring commentary, Minn describes the amazing places, animals, and people he encounters on his journey. As a teen I read Mark Twain's *The Adventures of Huckleberry Finn* and visited Tom Sawyer Island at Disneyland . The seed planted by Minn was watered by Huck and I knew someday I would have a Mississippi River "adventure".

Learn: As a college professor it was time for a "sabbatical"; a time to rest, renew and learn. My theme of "Creation Care: Environmental Justice" involved extensive reading in the field of Eco-Theology /Ethics(Larry

Rasmussen) and Literature (Wendell Berry). It would also involve study to become a Master Gardener. But because we learn best by "doing" I decided to "do" a paddling trip with the river as my "laboratory" so that I might learn about water, soil, and creatures … including humans.

Pilgrimage: As a boy my family went on annual "road-trips". I remember vividly many of the people and places. I was shaped in significant ways by those journeys. From ancient times people have made pilgrimages or "sacred journeys". Venturing forth from the familiar into the unknown invites an openness to the deeper, spiritual levels of life. As a paddling "pilgrim" I looked forward to how God would renew my spirit as each new day dawned and as I paddled around each bend in the river.

While much of my journey was "solo" I soon learned that I wasn't alone. A huge debt of gratitude is due to the many authors/guides/coaches that helped me prepare for the paddle pilgrimage, the countless "river angels" who fed, sheltered, and encouraged me along the way, and to my family in Washington State whose prayers sustained me the entire way. Special thanks to:

Holling Clancy Holling, author of *Minn of the Mississippi*, a beautiful illustrated book recounting a turtle's journey down the river.

Mark Twain, author of *The Adventures of Huckleberry Finn*, a groundbreaking adventure novel exploring the racial and moral universe of the late 19th century.

Eddy Harris, author of *Mississippi Solo: A Memoir*, a beautifully written account of a young African American and a "novice paddler's" journey down river into the South.

Bruce Nelson, author and adventurer, whose exploits *Walking across Alaska* and *Paddling the River* and website/blog www.bucktrack.com, have provided inspiration and practical advice.

Jeff Pearson, fellow Folbot paddler, for his detailed "tips" from his recent journey and helping outfit my boat with "loaned" equipment....www.deltaserf.com

Jim Lewis, author of *Ka-Ka-Ska-Ska ("Headwaters to the Gulf" – in a kayak)*, for his informative and entertaining account of paddling the river and for his hospitality in "launching" me on my paddle and coaching me from the headwaters to Minneapolis.

Pilgrimage is a quest for knowledge. Asking questions along the way helps the pilgrim to see more clearly and more deeply.

-Herb Brokering

He ordered them to take nothing for their journey except a staff; no bread, no bag, no money in their belts; but to wear sandals and not to put on two tunics.

Mark 6:8-9

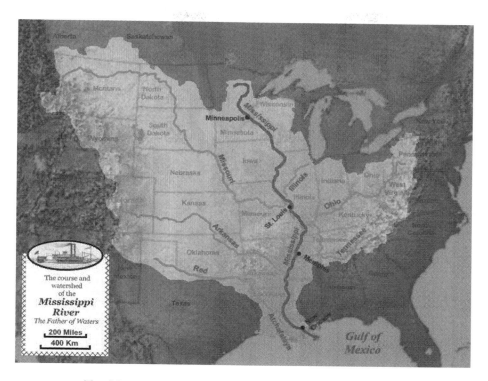

THE MISSISSIPPI RIVER DRAINS 40% OF THE CONTINENTAL U.S.

Bringing Back the White Pine

Even before the paddle began an important river experience occurred. The Mississippi River and its tributaries played an important role after settlers came to Northern Minnesota. These water highways provided a convenient way to transport a valuable "product": timber. These verdant arboreal forests abounded in White Pine. The "Queen of the Forest" produced the beautiful, clear, blond wood used to finish the interiors of homes. Like the "gold rush" in the Klondike, Minnesota's North Woods drew lumbermen to harvest this precious resource. Sadly, most of the White Pine was clear-cut and few of these majestic trees remain. Fortunately there is a "voice in the wilderness". Jack Rajala, a fourth generation forester, was inspired by his college biology professor to think beyond immediate economic gain.

One cannot with impunity rob Mother Nature of her treasures, for truly the sins of the fathers are avenged unto the third and fourth generation.

Dr. Agnes Larson

I had an opportunity to visit the Rajala estate by Wolf Lake near Park Rapids, MN, where Jack has made his life mission the restoring of this almost extinct "pillar of the forest".

His book, *Bringing Back The White Pine*, describes the challenges he has faced and the fascinating history of the logging industry in this region. One story stands out. A single family-owned company had the biggest local impact. They moved to Minnesota when they had exhausted the New England forests. Once the white pine forests were gone, they moved west to Washington my home state. Does the Weyerhauser name sound familiar? Stopped by the Pacific Ocean and guided by an enlightened forest management philosophy, replanting has largely replaced clear-cutting. Fortunately, individuals like Jack Rajala are busy replanting the North Woods.

Jack with White Pine seedling

The "headwaters" of the Mississippi River in early May.

Glorious it is when wandering time is come.

Eskimo Song

RIVER SCHOOL: HEADWATERS TO MINNEAPOLIS

Portage Pilgrim

"The practice of carrying water craft or cargo over land, either around an obstacle in a river, or between two bodies of water" That's what the dictionary says. Signs along the river give a suggestive visual.

We can thank the French fur-trappers for what should be pronounced "portaaaje" not the shortened Anglicized "portage". I have carried a canoe as pictured on my shoulders portaaaajing between lakes in Minnesota's Boundary Waters. But on the Mississippi the experience is more unpacking, slogging, dragging, and repacking. In the early going the portage was often a short journey around a fallen tree or shallow water through knee-deep muck which threatened to suck my neoprene booties off my feet. Chilled to the bone I felt little pain. Only later did I discover that my calf was twice its normal size due to a torn muscle requiring a hospital visit and a month wearing a compression sock.

Further downstream are several dams to portage around. The maps invariably pegged the distance of the portage at 300 yards. That doesn't sound too bad. The maps, however, didn't show that these little adventures would involve unpacking and hauling all the gear and then dragging my kayak through woods, across roads, into towns, and up and down steep embankments. If only I had brought along my kayak "caddy" to wheel the whole kit-and-kaboodle. Fortunately, my paddling buddy, Jim Lewis, helped me create a sling which I could throw over my shoulder to aid in dragging the boat. Several of the portages were much longer distances. A frequent portage companion was "rain". A few weeks later, as I relaxed downriver in my kayak and descended effortlessly in one of the 29 locks which bypass dams beyond Minneapolis, I began to appreciate all the hard work upriver as a Portage Pilgrim.

Watch and Pray....

Usually this dictum of Jesus is applied to "being ready" for what is called the "second coming" or as counsel in "avoiding temptation". These words kept echoing in my mind as I paddled the river. The natural environment suggested another interpretation. One has much to "watch" along the way.

You had better pay attention to the river for potential hazards like rocks and fallen trees called "sweepers", changes in the current, and channels that turn out to be dead ends. Vigilance is vital in monitoring the weather for wind direction and velocity, storms, heat, and cold fronts. A delightful watching discovers surprises around each bend as deer, raccoons, trumpeter swans, eagles, butterflies, geese and goslings, pelicans, and otters appear suddenly.

In the twists and turns of the river, watching and studying the maps is essential to making safe progress downstream. Finally, with hours of solo time, one can't avoid the "inward glance," taking a long and hard look at my own life. As I watched hour after hour my reflections flowed into prayer effortlessly, even gracefully.

Too often our prayers become a chore and hard work. On the river I have been reminded that if we "watch" and pay attention more carefully to our surroundings, prayer comes naturally as a wonderful gift.

How we listen, and do, and pray becomes the map we make.

Murray Bodo

There's a hole in the bucket

It seemed like such a good idea. I could fold up my Folbot kayak into a backpack and carry it wherever I traveled. I imagined taking it on adventures to the whale-calving bays of Baja and my ancestral fjords in Norway. It's zippered and Velcro deck compartments made for easy stowage of large quantities of needed gear. Its bright orange color was not only a good safety precaution but also just looked cool! Yes, there were limitations; maybe even cautionary clues to potential problems. The rudder assemblage was balky and making sharp, quick turns nearly impossible.

The spray skirt designed to protect me and the cockpit from unwelcome waves leaked. And finally the rubberized bottom seemed vulnerable to sharp objects on the river bottom. But I had trained in the *Leila V. I* and as legendary Texas football coach once said, "You gotta dance with the girl that brung you..."

So off we went from Lake Itasca. It had been an unusual spring in the upper Midwest with a modest snow cover melting a month early and ice leaving the lakes by mid-April. That meant several things: lakes and rivers would be clear for paddling, the water would be cold, and most important, water levels would be low. Standing knee deep in frigid water at the headwaters I experienced all three conditions. Cool weather and clear skies, however, made for an ideal launch. However, the narrow channel and shallow water soon made navigation difficult. The excitement of beginning the trip and attendant adrenaline won the day. Then we began to enter miles of bogs and marshes through which the river wound its serpentine path. I noticed that my buddy Jim's boat was gracefully tracking around the corners while I battled to make turns with constant paddle corrections. Numerous adjustments to the rudder made only minimal improvements in navigation. The extra paddling required during 10-12 hour days on the river, left weary and aching muscles as we set up camp each night.

One of the great benefits of kayaking is being able to paddle in shallow water. A boat with a deeper keel would run aground in much of the water we traversed. But this year's low water made even kayaking a challenge. Much of the bottom was sand and mud, but frequently fallen trees provided obstacles with sharp branches just below the surface ready to snag an unwary traveler. Patches of rock and gravel created a painful grinding sound and abrasive scratching of the boat's belly. Here and there large boulders left millennia ago by glacial action hid just below the surface ready to take a bite out of my bottom. But we made it through the most hazardous conditions and seemed on our way to the bigger water with its new challenges.

One afternoon as I paddled along there seemed to be more water in the bottom of my boat than usual. Pulling over to the side to pump out the water I tipped my boat over and discovered a small hole just below my cockpit. As I took out my repair kit to patch the leak I reached for my phone to call Jim, who had paddled ahead. But my phone wasn't in my life jacket pocket where I had put it. Apparently as I had exited the boat several times that day to walk it through shallow water, my cell phone had fallen out. Running along the shoreline downstream I called out to Jim. After about a mile I found him pulled to the side waiting for me. Working together we placed one large patch and several smaller patches on holes and dangerous points of abrasion. Fortunately, the weather was warm and sunny, so off we went.

The river bottom continued to scrape, scratch, and grab the bottom of my boat as we headed for a series of large lakes in the river, but the patches held. After crossing Lake Bemidji I pulled the boat out of the water on a boat ramp to inspect the bottom. I found the largest patch running along the keel line was slowly peeling off, but seemed secure enough to keep going. However, the really big lakes, Cass and Winnibigoshish were still ahead.

As we entered Wolf Lake, we were met with a strong headwind stirring billowing whitecaps. We gathered our strength behind a wall of reeds and prepared to battle the waves. Jim was off first and plowed ahead fearlessly. As soon I hit the lake a large wave washed across my bow and snuck into my cockpit through my faulty spray skirt. The 50 degree water took my breath away. I instantly knew that the Leila V. I wouldn't make it. I scurried back behind the reeds and called out to Jim to join me. Within minutes we knew I needed to replace my boat and began considering options.

Jim later confessed he had wondered if my Foldboat would be able to make the journey safely down the Mississippi, but he had decided to let the River answer that question. We now had an answer.

Two days later after a quick trip up into the Iron Range, we traded in the *Leila V.* I and purchased the *Leila V. II* from Jim's good friend, Chuck Newberg, at Spring Creek Outfitters in Mt. Iron.

My new boat a Wilderness System Tsunami 175, would serve me well for the rest of my pilgrimage.

Plan carefully and prepare to change all your plans.

Richard Swanson

The water was shrouded in drifting mist. A gradual crescendo of birds was warming their voices. The dawn of a new day suffused the horizon with an orange hue. My paddle dipped noiselessly and my kayak carved a clean slice in the dark water. The primal rays illumined the distant shore. The pulsing orb rose above the tree line and the river was bathed in umber as the mist swirled and melted around me.

A voice sang in my head. It was Curly singing praise to an Oklahoma daybreak.

"Oh, what a beautiful morning, oh what a beautiful day, I've got a wonderful feeling, everything's going my way. Oh, the sounds of the earth are like music, the sounds of the earth are like music, the breeze is so busy it don't miss a tree, and an old weeping willow is laughing at me. All the cattle are standing like statues, all the cattle are standing like statues, the corn is as high as an elephant's eye, and a little brown maverick is winking her eye."

And I had no choice but to join in the chorus, "Oh, what a beautiful morning, Oh, what a beautiful day, I've gotta wonderful feeling, everything's going my way!"

SUNSET OVER "BIG WINNIE"

I could have killed him!

One of the delights of paddling in Minnesota is its Water Only Accessible Campgrounds. These campgrounds are maintained by the DNR (Department of Natural Resources), and are identified on an excellent series of 9 maps. These maps are gold as they share vital information for the journey about historic points of interest, flora and fauna, and river conditions. Jim and I regularly consulted these maps, which I kept on the dashboard of the Leila V II, and planned our day's travel to arrive at a campground before nightfall. For the most part the camp grounds were in scenic locations, well-maintained and occasionally even provided a much appreciated rustic shelter from rain or snow.

DEPARTMENT OF NATURAL RESOURCES (DNR) WATER-ACCESSIBLE CAMPGROUND

Spying the camp marker became one of the most eagerly anticipated sights each evening. From time to time, however, locating the camp was a challenge as trees and undergrowth camouflaged the take-out from our vision. On a few occasions when no campground was to be found we watched for an occasional narrow cement boat ramp where we could drag out kayaks out of the river. This was one of those nights.

A storm was approaching and we were dog-tired after a long day on the river. We got our tents set up on a grassy area and were asleep within a few minutes when the storm hit. And it rained and rained ... Fortunately thus far on our trip the weather, though often cold and sometimes rainy, was remarkably favorable. In the early going there were a few frosty nights, but by mid-morning, the sun was usually out and the skies clear. Waking from time to time during the night I was grateful to be snug in my sleeping bag as the rain hit "rat-a-tat" on my tent's rain-fly. Jim's voice was my alarm-clock as he called out "Are you awake?" As I rubbed my eyes in the dawn's early light I immediately heard a now familiar sound. It was raining and raining hard! Naively I answered that I was awake and wondered out-loud "Are we starting out now.....in the rain!" To which Jim simply said, "Of course, and it won't be the last time!" Jim was already dismantling his tent as I grumpily gathered my gear inside my tent.

Frankly, the thought of breaking camp and paddling in the cold rain wasn't what I had planned for when I signed on for this journey. I was ready to stay in my tent until the rain stopped. When I got all my gear together and down to the river, Jim was already in his boat and eager to get going. As my numb fingers fumbled with hatch covers, he announced that he was heading out and he would see me downriver in Palisade. By this point I was actually relieved to see him leave.

The map told me it was a three hour paddle to this town. This was a section of river with many twists and turns. It was soon clear that I would have to summon every ounce of will-power to keep going. A blast of rain coming sideways greeted me as I came around a bend driving me to hug the shelter of the shore. Even with my rain gear and spray skirt snugly in place I was soon completely wet and cold to the bone. When I would get

to the lee-ward shore in the wind-shadow I found that I could tuck my chin into my hood and blow warm air down into my jacket providing a small measure of relief before the wind would blast me again around the next bend. Now was the time to have no wasted motion and to paddle as efficiently as possible. Remembering Jim's instruction that pushing the paddle was a more effective way to paddle, I began chanting out loud as I stroked "Push forward, pull back" and kept this cadence as my mantra for good stretches of river. Then the cold would win and my stroke would fall apart and it felt like I was fighting the water.

My appreciation for Jim's coaching was morphing into anger for his dragging me out in these miserable conditions. Perhaps anger is not the most noble of motivators, but it served me well as I continued to battle my way toward Palisade. Jim had mentioned that we would have breakfast there. That promise proved to be another motivation pulling me forward. I found myself imagining a warm restaurant and eggs, hash brown potatoes, toast, orange juice, and coffee.

I was completely numb when I finally arrived at a small park on the edge of the tiny town. I expected Jim to be waiting for me, but he was nowhere to be found. Like a shark drawn to blood in the water, I made a dash toward what looked like Main Street. Passing a church I was tempted to go inside hoping that coffee hour had started. Still wearing my spray skirt, I decided not to test the local Lutheran hospitality, and stumbled toward the only café in town. As I opened the door I was hit with the warm blast of air laden with the heavenly scent of breakfast followed by a familiar voice, "Where have you been, I have been waiting for you".

Sitting by the door was Jim with a tall pile of hot pancakes and bacon, juice and steaming coffee arrayed before him. As I peeled off my layers of wet clothes and hung them by the heater, he asked, "How are you doing?" My "better self" was absent as I blurted out, "I am terrible! I have never had such a miserable morning in my life! I am contemplating a criminal act......killing you!"

He laughed and began describing how good the food was and that I should sit down and enjoy myself. About an hour later with a full belly and having regained feeling in my fingers and toes, I reluctantly abandoned my murder plot. Fortunately the rain had stopped when we got back on the river, but I think Jim kept a cautious eye on me from then on lest he become a victim of a suspicious death. Now many months later I look back and recognize this miserable morning as another important lesson that my buddy and the river had taught me about pushing through difficult times. And there would be more to come.....

21

MAPPING THE DAY'S PADDLE

Surfing Big Winnie

The Upper Mississippi has a number of unusual features. It flows north for its first 160 miles before finally beginning its southern descent. The river frequently changes course in its upper reaches as it passes through bogs and marshes. These twists and turns and bends often mean paddling many miles to actually travel a relatively short distance "as the crow flies".

A favorite feature to fishermen is a number of lakes that are a part of the river. The biggest and most famous is Lake Winnibigoshish, or "Big Winnie" as the locals call it. With 140 miles of pristine, undeveloped shoreline its waters teem with Walleye, Northern Pike, Bass, and Crappie. One would think an open expanse of water would be a welcome sight after mile upon mile of serpentine meandering. As we approached Big Winnie we had to paddle across Cass Lake where I relived childhood memories visiting my Great Uncle August's shoreline cabin. But Big Winnie was another story. On the DNR maps it appeared like a huge aneurysm in the blood stream. In bold print was a warning to not venture across its 13 mile expanse because sudden winds could stir its relatively shallow waters into a seething mass. Map warning duly noted.

We reached BW on the Opening Day of fishing season; a day in Minnesota rivaling major holidays. Despite relatively clear weather, we didn't see the normal high volume of boats. A small armada huddled on the leeward side of the lake avoiding what appeared to be a modest breeze. As a precaution we donned our wetsuits and secured our spray skirts. The water temperature was in the low 40's. Our plan was a conservative one as we "tacked" for points of land we could see in the distance. Looking across the lake's widest expanse, I remembered as a child first gazing on the ocean, and not seeing the far shore, I shuddered. Big Winnie had earned her name. As we cautiously crept along the shoreline sheltered from the wind, we approached the fleet of fishermen. The ripple of wind on the surface was just beyond. As we contemplated our next "tack" a few of the boaters gave us an understated Minnesota wave which seemed to betray a look of skepticism about the wisdom of these kayakers.

At this point I looked to Jim for what we would do next. He had paddled across Big Winnie several times before, so I trusted his judgment. Finally, he said, "Let's do it!" We headed out across the broadest stretch of water I had ever attempted to cross. At first we were buoyed by the exhilaration of being pushed along by a modest "tail-wind". We were making good time. Almost before we knew it the wind picked up, just as the maps had warned. Excitement turned to apprehension and anxiety, as gentle waves grew into larger swells. Soon we were "surfing" down large waves and had all we could do to keep our kayaks pointing straight ahead. Were we to have gotten "sideways" our boats would have capsized and in these conditions we would likely perish in the frigid water. We also had reached a point of "no-return".

Jim was a stronger and more efficient paddler and had a more stream-lined boat. He shouted to me over the wind that he had to keep moving ahead or he would be in danger of tipping. Slowly his boat pulled ahead of mine. Fortunately he was wearing his yellow reflective vest as the afternoon progressed, the distance between boats grew, and the dusk began to descend.

I continued to battle onward remembering his upriver paddling advice to try to paddle a couple miles an hour faster than the current. He had explained that I needed to be "in control" instead of the river. That certainly was the case now as the wind howled and the waves continued to grow lifting me high before descending at dizzying speed.

Before long Jim's boat was a small yellow dot in the distance. Every few minutes a rogue wave would push try to push me sideways and I fought to keep the Leila V II at a right angle downwind to the wave. The yellow dot that was Jim disappeared as I dipped into a deep trough. Cresting the next wave I peered ahead squinting through water-drenched glasses hoping to locate the rapidly diminishing yellow dot. It seemed like hours had passed. In truth nearly two hours had gone by since we had ventured onto Big Winnie. I wondered if I would survive. This would be an embarrassing way to die. Maybe the people who had thought this river pilgrimage was crazy were right. I never had doubted that this was a bit crazy, but now I admitted feeling a bit foolish.

But I had no choice. I had to paddle on! About the time that my friend Jim's yellow dot disappeared, something different began to appear. It was the other shore or at least the point of land we were "making for". However, would the wind blow me past that point out into another large stretch of lake whose shore was barely visible?

I am not sure what happened next or why, but as I paddled, I began to feel less anxious and more at ease negotiating the wind and waves. Perhaps it was exhaustion fueled by adrenaline and a small bit of newly acquired skill and confidence, but I sensed I would survive. This unexpected surfing expedition became surprisingly fun, and for the next half-hour I cautiously celebrated my passage through the waters.

Jim had been worriedly waiting for me when I finally paddled my boat into the calm waters. Then it hit me, the intoxicating smell of food cooking at a resort along the lake's edge. My body was limp, my mind empty, but my spirit soared as we pulled our boats out of the water and headed for dinner.

As we ate, Jim asked me, "How big do you think the waves were?" "Maybe 7 feet?"

"I think they were 8 footers!" He sheepishly added, "We should have never gone out in those condition … don't tell my wife. I will be in big trouble. I could have drowned, but she would have never forgiven me if I had taken you out and you had lost your life."

As we crawled into our tent that night, I realized how foolish we had been to tempt Big Winnie, but I was also thrilled that we had done it. I knew I wouldn't face any more difficult conditions for the rest of my pilgrimage.

That which does not kill us makes us stronger.

Friedrich Nietzsche

Paddling for peace

One of the most beautiful stretches of the river flows between Brainerd and Little Falls, MN. The current dances over the rocky bottom, the verdant forest hugs the banks, and wildlife plays on the surface and in the sky.

My morning reverie was suddenly interrupted by several huge explosions. When I consulted my map I discovered I was traveling through the Camp Ripley Military Reservation. I flashed back to a boyhood memory of passing army convoys and waving to the young soldiers. For the next two hours I was surrounded by the percussion of artillery fire and the staccato of gunfire.

A thought crossed my mind...."we have entered civilization..." I reflected on the enormous expenditures of dollars and lives on war that could be used for "peacemaking". I thought of St. Francis and his life which actively sought peace and care of creation. And I was reminded how we are all called to that noble task.

The end of the human race will be that it will eventually die of civilization.

Ralph Waldo Emerson

Learning from the Master

When I read *Ka-Ka-Ska-Ska*, which documents author/adventurer, Jim Lewis' journey down the Mississippi, I knew I had to meet him and pick his brain. Little did I know that he and his wife, Sharron, would welcome me into their home and that he would paddle with me from the headwaters to Minneapolis. In those three weeks he would teach me about paddling, camping, planning, safety, and savoring the journey. One "grows with the river" but Jim's coaching has prepared me for not only this trip but for life itself.

HEARTLAND:
MINNEAPOLIS TO ST. LOUIS

All's well...

Well, the day didn't start out so well. Night-time torrential rains had closed Minneapolis' St. Anthony Falls lock to recreational craft and I had to be towed back up-stream to Boom Island by a friendly boater. Fortunately, Todd, my local host, came to my rescue and hauled me and the *Leila V. II* downriver to the start of Lake Pepin near Red Wing, MN. Apparently I had rescued Todd as well from helping pack relatives for a move.

Lake Pepin is the largest "lake" on the Mississippi often over a mile wide and 23 miles from end to end. As a boy I had fished for walleye pike on this body of water with my dad and Uncle Les. I remembered it as one of the most beautiful stretches of the Mississippi. Framed by majestic limestone bluffs its shores are dotted with little towns. But this river-carved valley can also become a wind-tunnel producing hazardous conditions on the water.

It was now early afternoon and a light breeze brought relief from the heat and humidity. These were ideal conditions for safe passage down the lake to the town of Pepin and dinner at the famous Harbor View Cafe. It seemed like my fortunes had turned around as I steadily paddled downstream. Having spent several weeks on the river, I should have known that the weather can change quickly. The breeze had grown into a steady wind which soon was whipping up white caps. It was becoming clear that I wouldn't make it to Pepin.

My maps showed the town of Stockholm, WI downriver and across the lake. I hugged the Minnesota side until I was directly across the lake and with a strong tail-wind tacked for my new destination. The wind continued to accelerate until I was surfing down 4-5 foot waves. Using my Big Winnie surfing skills I virtually flew across the water.

In the distance I could see people sitting in lawn chairs by the beach at a camp ground. I decided that was my best place to land. Paddling with all my might I topped a large wave and was carried far up on the beach coming to rest right in front of an enthusiastic audience. They responded to my performance with applause and cheers. Greatly relieved, I sat panting in my boat, as someone shouted, "Did you plan to land here?" Little did they know that none of the day's adventure had gone as planned.

AMY, JANET, SUZANNE

Evening brought a welcome stay at the wonderful old Victorian home of friends who had once owned the Harbor View Cafe. Safe from the howling winds I slept like a baby. I awoke to the wind whistling through the trees- not a good sign. Making my way down to the Lake, I found the same wind stirring frothy waves and pushing swells far up on the beach. As I walked back through the quaint little village center, the sun was coming up and fluffy clouds floated overhead. Sitting on a bench in the early morning rays I waited for the Bogus Creek Café and Bakery to open for breakfast. It became my snug harbor where I hung out all day eating, writing in my blog, and chatting with the locals. From time to time I would venture out to see if I could launch my boat. As this restful day wore on, I was glad to be shanghaied in such a peaceful and lovely place.

While the food at Bogus Creek was excellent, the highlight of my stay was to be found elsewhere. Upon entering the town the previous night, a brightly-colored corner building had caught my eye-the Stockholm Pie Company.

During the day I stopped in several times to case the joint. A rose-cheeked blond, blue-eyed woman named Janet cheerily told me that she had baked 40 pies that day and that business had been steady. Growing up in the Midwest in largely Scandinavian communities I had come to love a good home-baked pie. I was fortunate to stop in just before closing time, because 39 ½ pies had been consumed. Only one half of a berry pie remained. Having lost nearly 30 pounds on my trip thus far, I certainly needed to replace calories. And what better way to do it but to enjoy half a pie. Janet asked if I wanted my pie ala mode. Absolutely! That was a no-brainer. As she began to lock up she invited me to stay as long as I wanted. I have never tasted a better pie in my life. "All"s well that ends well!"

Letter to the River

Dear Miss,

I hope you are not offended by my familiar or even intimate form of address, but after nearly a month together I feel we have grown quite close. Each day as I begin my paddle you greet me and I discover something new about your personality. While I am only a beginner, you have been greeting others for thousands of years. You have become my teacher and I have learned many lessons. Some I have welcomed, others have been hard and painful. You have taught me with the rich diversity of your path from marshes to pine forests, across large lakes, through farmland, along majestic bluffs, through maze-like bayous, by small towns, suburbs, and cities, over wing dams and through locks and dams. I have studied with eagles, trumpeter swans, geese, ducks, deer, otter, beaver, pelican, and, yes, mosquito. I have been humbled by your twists and turns, eddies, sweepers and whirlpools and exhilarated by your rapids, tail-winds, and strong flow after a rain. My sore hands, aching back, stiff knees, flagging frame, and frequently struggling spirit all remind me of my limits, my age, and my mortality. But that is good, because you teach with a clarity and truth that I need to hear and embrace. And while I may curse you with some regularity I praise you for the "wisdom" you invite me into each morning as I set out from your shores. Roll on, mighty waters!

Your humble "Paddle Pilgrim"

"Come forth into the light of things. Let Nature be your teacher."

-William Wordsworth

Summertime

Another musical I have always loved is Porgy and Bess. While the characters are a bit stereotyped, the music still moves me.

"Summer time and the livin' is easy.......fish are jumping and the cotton is high." I now understand that line "fish are jumpin'.." because they really do jump all the time and all over the river. Maybe it's because I am on the water all day and have little else to do, but here's the best part of a "true story". On several occasions fish have jumped over the front of my boat and almost jumped into my boat. My uncle Lester is smiling and nodding his head! And they do this without warning often causing a spike in my blood pressure and other near anatomical responses.

In local riverside restaurants the fish list jumps off the menu. In Minnesota, the walleye heads the list. But down in the lower Mississippi, you can choose between catfish, buffalo, and carp. Being a vegetarian I am certainly a "stranger in a strange land". Despite her sweet intentions, I had to tell a waitress recently that "fried okra" was not the solution.

Never eat more than you can lift.

Miss Piggy

Fishing, Technology, and Uncle Lester

Have you noticed lately how high tech has invaded the world of fishing? Is my bias showing? As I have paddled through stretches of Wisconsin, Minnesota, and Iowa I have seen lots of "gear" on fishing boats to help anglers find and catch fish.

There is some good news to report, however, as I hear of lots of "catch and release" fishing. Perhaps I am old school, but I thought fishing was about learning where the "holes" were by years of studying their habits, trial and error on the water, and fish-tales from old-timers. Satellites that can follow my movements from space scare me and give me some compassion for my brothers and sisters underwater trying to elude "fish-finders" from above.

One of my dad's 10 sibs was Lester. Uncle Les was the family fish guru. Picture a round, rosy-cheeked, white haired man with a straw hat and bib overalls. Lester was a rural mail-carrier primarily so he could fish after delivering the mail. Two of his sons became college professors, so he was a smart fellow. But his "applied" study was the life and habits of fish within 50 miles of Decorah, Iowa. As I paddled through that stretch of water recently, the spirit of Uncle Lester and I communed. I'm not kidding!

He knew where the crappies, walleye, and striped bass all lived because he spent time on the Mississippi. The river and its creatures had been his teachers. I took my son, Erik, to visit Decorah one summer to meet Uncle

Les. I knew this master fisherman would deliver the goods where his father had generally failed. So off we went to the river. He asked, "Erik, what do you want to catch?" Erik replied, "Anything!"

My son, Erik, and Uncle Lester

Off we went to one "hole" after another. In every case we caught a lot of fish. Erik was amazed. But I wasn't surprised, because I knew that my uncle was a real fisherman who did it the "old-fashioned" way.

Guttenberg, Iowa

Even though I had lived in Iowa during high school and college, I didn't know much about this town with the curious name. For starters the correct pronunciation is not Goootenberg, but Gut-as in your belly-berg. The only other Guttenberg I knew of was the German inventor of the printing press which revolutionized communication in the 1400's. This town of largely German immigrants, named after the same Johannes Guttenberg, is a picturesque village with many lovely stone buildings quarried from the limestone bluffs along the river. It is also the site of Lock and Dam #10. Another long day of paddling was drawing to a close as I "locked through" at Guttenberg and began to think about where I might camp for the night.

As I cleared the turbulent water below the dam I found myself in a back-water with a small sandy beach. Two people were standing on the beach. I began my regular litany, "Hi, I'm Dave and I am paddling the river......" I had to be quick as the current was strong and I could see that I would soon pass the edge of town and be back in the main channel lined with high banks and dense woods. I blurted, "Are there any good campground nearby?" The gentleman said, "No, but you are welcome to pull up on the beach and stay here."

Already downstream I dug hard with my paddle and returned dragging the *Leila V. II* up onto a small patch of white sand. He introduced himself as John and his daughter, Ashley, and told me that they had hosted other paddlers over the years as they had come down the river. On one of those occasions a group of paddlers from around the world had stayed on this little spit of land. Mentioning that I hadn't seen many sandy beaches along the Upper Mississippi, he explained that the sand I was standing on was actually ground-up shells used to make buttons at a factory nearby.

As I began to notice my surroundings John told me that he and his daughter were teachers. Behind John were a series of old dilapidated buildings that hugged the shoreline. Several small boats were clustered around a covered lean-to with what appeared to be a bait-tanks and a fish cleaning table. He explained that the buildings were fishing shacks that his grandfather and father had used in their family "catfish" operation. Some fishing was still happening but it was now more of a hobby and he used the shack to come and relax and have a beer. Ashley told me that her dad was a local amateur historian who served on the city council. I had certainly come to the right place and met the right folks!

When I asked where I should set up my tent, John insisted I crash in one of the fishing shacks.

THE GUTTENBERG HILTON

The shack's rustic interior walls were covered with Iowa Hawkeye sports posters and a neon beer sign that I guess may have been "lifted" during those same college years. A small table and a bar and a large bed made my new digs the Guttenberg "Hilton". As my hosts departed they wished me safe travels and I headed up the hill into town for a very welcome dinner and early turn-in.

Up at dawn and back into town for breakfast at a small "Ma and Pa" Diner, I enjoyed my meal as a parade of locals came in, gave Midwest "nods" of greeting, and bantered with each other and the matronly waitress. Most of the chatter was about fishing. Sitting in a back booth was the local priest who smiled a gracious blessing as each of the fishermen headed out with apologies for missing Mass.

As I walked back along the street toward my boat, a car pulled up along-side. My first instinct was the police were checking on this suspicious-looking character sauntering through their quiet town.

Instead it was my new friend, John. Leaning out the window and extend-ing his hand he said, "I was on my way to Mass and decided to stop by to see how you were doing….." I thanked him for his hospitality and that I would never forget my stay in Guttenberg. I told him how glad I was to see him and, "the priest will be happy to see someone in church with most of the town out fishing!"

On pilgrimage the stranger becomes a saintly figure.

Brett Webb-Mitchell

O River of Change

Have you noticed how the Mississippi River has changed? A little stream has become a massive body of water coursing toward the Gulf of Mexico.

Since Minneapolis I have "locked thru" scores of Army Corps of Engineers locks and dams. Usually my little kayak is the only boat as the water goes down. Minnesota, Wisconsin, and Iowa have all felt like home having lived and gone to college in this region. The Mississippi will run free and fast in Missouri and the "South."

But as the river has changed, the friendly people have been a constant and I don't think that will change. The great folks at the Keokuk Yacht Club invited me to rest and celebrate with food, drink, and shelter. Robbie even called ahead to his buddies down river in Quincy to let them know I was coming. I couldn't tell if he was pulling my leg, when he asked as I departed, "Have you seen the movie, "Deliverance"?

ROBBIE AND CHARLIE AT THE KEOKUK YACHT CLUB

THE WELCOMING COMMITTEE AT THE QUINCY BOAT CLUB: MARK, DAVE, AND PHIL

A Math Question

Most days I paddle a minimum of 10 hours. The other day I was in my kayak for 13 hours. As I move through the lower Mississippi after St. Louis there are no dams/locks as the flow of the river picks up speed. I plan to paddle 50 plus miles each day. There are fewer towns and bigger barges. It's a big river as it moves into the "South".

So here's a math question I thought of during one of the more monotonous stretches of the river. How many strokes of my paddle will be required to get me to New Orleans?

a. 750,000

b. 6,000,000

c. 2,000,000

d. 3,500,000

I will spare you the math calculations. But at a rate of 50-60 strokes per minute, 10 hours a day, 65 days of paddling......the correct answer is approximately 2,000,000.

Now I will do my best to wipe that information out of my mind!

LOWER MISSISSIPPI: ST. LOUIS TO MEMPHIS

MID-MISSISSIPPI: GATEWAY TO THE WEST *AND* THE SOUTH

"There ain't nothing down there."

That's what Ray had told me when I left the last "fuel dock" just south of St. Louis. I had heard variations on that theme from others.

LOW WATER EXPOSES "WING DAM" IN LOWER MISSISSIPPI

Jeff told me to have at least 5 gallons of water on board south of Memphis because towns were few and far between and temperatures and humidity would soar, and was he right! Others were probably referring to how the Upper Mississippi's wildlife is so abundant and its shores so scenic. The Lower Mississippi is a persistent montage of sand bars and rip-wrap levees protecting occasional hamlets and farms. My conclusion, however, is that it's simply different down here. The sand bars make for great beach camp sites. The critters may be a bit more ornery (gar, water moccasins, alligators). But the folks north AND south have been very helpful and friendly. So, Ray, there's lots down here, with surprises around each bend of the river.

If I take the wings of the morning and settle at the farthest limits of the sea, even there your hand shall lead me, and your right hand shall hold me fast.

Psalm 139:9

The best beer....ever

I knew that the farther I traveled down the river it would get hotter. Each day I listened on my marine radio to weather forecasts from NOAA (National Oceanic and Atmospheric Administration). In the early going it was amusing to hear the distinctly Norwegian brogue accent in the voice of the weather forecaster. Almost perfect warm summer days arrived as I passed the verdant green hills and bluffs through northern Iowa under fluffy white clouds. A series of hot dry days with strong headwinds signaled a change and as I paddled through Illinois I began to hear forecasts which predicted unseasonably hot days....even record heat. I knew the drill. The key was to drink plenty of water. Fortunately I had my own portable "facilities" to handle over-hydration.

As the early June days came and I passed the mid-point of my journey at St. Louis the temperatures were averaging the mid 90's. I was typically carrying 5 gallons of fresh water with me which I regularly restocked. For a bit of variety I also kept a supply of electrolyte replacement drinks like Gatorade, Propel, PowerAde, and All Sport. I had been warned that south of St. Louis towns were less frequent, and keeping an adequate supply of fluids was vital. This prediction was confirmed at one of the last "marinas" near Kimmswick, MO.

As I hiked into the little town to grab a quick lunch, I passed a beautiful mansion on the river bank. A small sign identified it as the summer home of the Anheuser family. Anheuser? Of course, I thought, Anheuser-Busch was the company that produced Budweiser Beer. Countless ads helped me remember the message, "The beer that made St. Louis famous".

I had lunch in a delightful little restaurant topped off with a cold fresh-squeezed orange juice before heading back in the heat to my boat. I filled my water bottles. "There ain't nothin' down there...." echoed in my mind as I pushed off.

With a good flow I made excellent progress and at dusk pulled off the river at a campground with a boat launch and a small sandy beach. As I set up my tent I noticed several fishermen a ways up the beach. Hungry and tired I prepared dinner and was about to crawl into my tent, when one of the fishermen called out, "Hey, are you thirsty? Come on over and have a beer?" I didn't need to be asked twice.

Walking over to their campsite, Herb introduced himself, his two sons, Brady and Brandon, and their Jack Russell terrier, Mia.

Herb, Mia, Brady and Brandon near Wittenberg, MO.

He apologized for not being more hospitable as he handed me a tall chilled can of beer. Being from the Northwest I have to confess I have become a bit of a beer-snob who prefers micro-brews. The beer he handed me was cheap and cold but I can say without a shadow of a doubt that it was the best beer I have ever drunk.

The conversation was equally enjoyable as I told them about my trip and they shared about their lives. All the while they pulled in fish after fish. That was a story in itself. Hoping to land a big catfish, all that seemed to be biting were "Gar". Gar is a curious looking prehistoric fish whose long tooth-filled snout looks like a mini alligator. As soon as the boys had carefully detached the gar from their lines, Mia would fearlessly grab and ferociously shake it before carrying it off into a pile of gar being created behind a tree.

Delightfully entertained and sufficiently hydrated, I thanked my new friends and bid them "good night". Crawling into my tent I remembered the sign by the boat launch with the name of the town where I was staying. Martin Luther would have certainly enjoyed with me the beer and conversation in this place with the same name as his home, Wittenberg.

Heaven is a lake of beer and every sip a prayer.

Attributed to St. Brigid

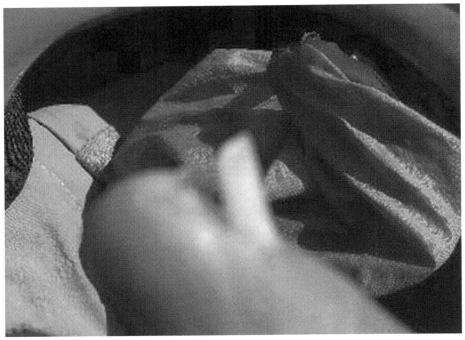

Guess what this is?

My little finger nail decided not to go to New Orleans

My hands were so cold in the early going that I didn't realize I had bent my nail so far back that it had broken and a month later.........eeewwwuuuu!

My radar don't show no fronts!

That's what a "good ol' boy" told me as he fished near Wittenberg, MO. Fishing chatter invariably involves weather prognostication. I was surprised by his sophisticated electronic forecast. I knew, however, from daily experience that I was in the midst of a hot and dry stretch with more to come. High water and flood stage last year was over 40 feet. It's currently 14 feet and going down. The emerging sand bars and wing dams are like sentinels along the river's path protecting and directing the flow. The air rippled in the heat above the current's surge. As I paddled away he shouted, "Be safe!"

Not more than an hour later I made one of my regular over-the-shoulder glances to see if a barge was sneaking up behind me. Instead I saw angry, gray and dark blue clouds were marching across the sky and pushing me down the river. A mixture of fear and excitement quickened my paddle stroke-count. I figured I could outrun the rain. Was I ever wrong. The wind picked up and with it I was bathed in a warm shower. This was a far cry from the precipitation back in Minnesota which chilled me to the bone. Just before I found my sand bar hotel, the storm was over. I guess the radar must have missed that one. I am glad I didn't.

Sunshine is delicious, rain is refreshing, wind braces us up, snow is exhilarating. There is really no such thing as bad weather; only different kinds of weather.

John Ruskin

River Angels

When I left Minneapolis I would be paddling solo. While my confidence and skill to navigate the river had grown enormously, I still wondered, "Can I do really this?" For the next two months I would be traveling all by myself in new territory populated largely by strangers. I had already begun to discover that river folks were different. While traveling years ago in the Middle-East I learned of the "law of the desert" which dictated that if a stranger was on your land at sunset it was your responsibility to treat them as a friend. I shouldn't have been surprised that the same rule of hospitality was at work along the river. Time and time again as I had need of shelter from a storm or food to sustain me or a place to lay my head, strangers became friends. More than friends, they became my river angels.

Do not forget to show hospitality to strangers, for some who have done this have shown hospitality to angels without knowing it.

Hebrews 13:2

AUNT ETHEL AND COUSIN GRETCHEN IN LACROSSE, WI.

Nathan and Phil at Ferryville, WI.

C Cathy near Brownsville, WI.

Nate, Andres and Diana in Dubuque, IA.

Barb at Bellevue, IL.

Nan at Muscatine, IA.

John and Bonnie in St. Charles, MO.

DEMETRIUS IN CAPE GIRARDEAU, MO.

LAURA AND "HOOK" IN CAIRO, IL.

RECCO, TRABIAS, AND AUNA IN NEW MADRID, MO.

NATE, MEGAN, AND JUSTIN IN CARUTHERSVILLE, MO.

BILLY, STEVE AND LLOYD IN CARUTHERSVILLE, MO.

MARK IN OSCEOLA, AR.

JIM, CHUCK, JASON AND DENNIS AT MUD ISLAND MARINA, MEMPHIS, TN.

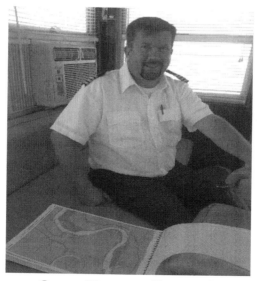

CAPTAIN MARK NEAR TUNICA, MS.

Nephew Billy in Greenville, MS.

The "Captain's Table" at Bellchase Marine Transport near New Orleans

And the Spirit immediately drove Jesus into the wilderness. He was in the wilderness forty days, tempted by Satan; and he was with the wild beasts, and the angels waited on him.

Mark 1:12

EMBRACING THE WILDERNESS: MEMPHIS TO NEW ORLEANS

The Solitude

DODGING STORMS ON A LOUISIANA SANDBAR

While I encounter people occasionally, most of the time I am alone. But am I? I am by myself, but I am not alone. I am surrounded by "clouds of witnesses". Each of you is with me in the most powerful and visceral way. Each morning I spend a good bit of time praying. Usually it is "out loud". I talk to God. I sing. I laugh. I weep. You are with me in the very deepest of senses.

Maybe the strangest and most wonderful part of my praying is conversations with dead people. I began talking to my dad who died several years ago. Then I thought of all the special people in my life who have passed, gone over, and entered glory. Since they don't weigh anything or take up space, they are now paddling partners on this pilgrimage.

One of my seminary professors/mentors was Henri Nouwen. He coined a phrase in one his books which captures the spirit of this third act of my river drama. I have moved from "loneliness to solitude".

Language has created the word loneliness to express the pain of being alone, the word solitude to express the glory of being alone.

Paul Tillich

River Cuisine

Since returning home many people have asked me what I ate on my trip. As with many facets of my pilgrimage, many changes occurred as I learned along the way. Almost as important as what I ate was where I ate. Location, location, location ruled. Weather also played a major role in my diet, as did the food-carrying capacity of my kayak.

Initially my plan was to prepare meals in camp in the morning and evening and to eat "on the fly" while paddling. Using my *Jet Boil* stove I could heat water and add it to oatmeal and coffee/cocoa for breakfast. On cold mornings near the headwaters, starting the day with a warm meal was essential and sent me off with food in my belly. On rainy/snowy mornings we were fortunate to have a shelter for our tents and protect us from the elements. Without a shelter we ate quickly and hit the river.

During the day I munched on healthy energy bars and found that Clif Bars were the most nutritious and contained the most calories. Calories, calories, calories! Paddling burns approximately 300 calories an hour especially in extreme weather conditions.

When we made camp at night in one of the many excellent "river-only" campgrounds maintained by the DNR, we had time to fix a more substantial meal. But often I was too pooped to create a really tasty meal. I soon discovered that the Knorr packaged meals (rice/beans/noodles) took a long time to fully soften, and I found myself crunching on half—cooked rice/noodles. They are also exceedingly salty. Jim's suggestion to add a bit of tobasco helped, but I had to force myself to consume an entire package.

Within a week I had to take up a notch in my belt. Jim reminded me regularly to keep eating and drinking, but I continued to lose weight. I figured I could afford to shed a few pounds. As I dutifully chowed down, Jim skillfully threw together gourmet meals. His favorite had to be creating scores of tiny pancakes with enough for snacking on throughout the morning.

My favorite came at the end of each day after we had cleaned up and were about to crawl into our tents. As the fire cracked Jim would ask, are you ready for the "Captain"? He would then pull out of his pack, a bottle of Captain Morgan Rum, and pour a snort into our coffee cups. A few sips of this elixir before sleep was a perfect end to a long day.

In Jim's book, *Ka-Ka-Ska-Ska*, he shared a dictum about nutrition. "If there is a restaurant or bar near the river, stop and eat." Given my weight-loss and hunger for real food, I took this advice to heart. As a result I can vividly remember, taste, and even smell the pizza near Big Winnie. Or the French fries on a frigid day in St. Cloud. Or several home-cooked meals at Jim and Sharron's home in Grand Rapids. Or frozen yogurt with fresh fruit and chocolate sprinkles with the Bueglers in Minneapolis. Or half of a triple-berry pie alamode in Stockholm, WI. You get my point.

Not only was I replacing needed carbohydrates but I was given "carte blanche" to eat as much as I wanted of almost anything. This epicurean dream became even more essential and enjoyable in the Lower Mississippi River. With towns few and far between, I relied for many days on a diet of Clif bars, mixed nuts, and energy drinks/water. I was able to occasionally get fresh fruit and keep it moderately cool in lower compartment below the water line of the *Leila V. II.*

But my real dietary salvation came from a surprising place: Casinos. From Illinois south a number of Casinos are found on River Boats or large hotel-like structures on the river banks.

ISLE OF CAPRI CASINO NEAR NATCHEZ, MS.

I remember reading about them but never realized what a God-send they would be.

Here's the drill. Exit the river; secure the boat at a dock, on a sand bar, or on the rocky shoreline; and trudge up to the Casino. As I approach the entrance, remember that I am looking like a hobo and probably smelling a bit rank after several days without a shower. Upon entrance greet the security staff and recite my litany, "Hi, I'm Dave and I am paddling down the entire Mississippi........" I now added a new line," I need to get out of the heat for a few hours and have a good meal....where is your buffet?" After they had looked me over, I would proceed with my backpack to the restroom and took a sink "shower".

As I progressed down the river I got bolder and bolder and eventually stripped off all my clothes and even washed them in the sink. The looks I got from customers who happened on a naked man in the restroom were priceless.

Refreshed and a bit cleaner I made my way to the buffet and plunked down my $10. I explained my situation to the Cashier, Maitre'd, and waitress; whereupon I was ushered to a table. Proceeding to the buffet I filled plates with salads, main courses, and desserts.

Covering a table with plates I offered a sincere "grace" and began a 2-3 hour feast. To be perfectly honest the hours I spent in 6-7 casinos were some of the best of the whole trip. The food tasted wonderful and despite my ragamuffin appearance, the waitresses were friendly and often asked about my trip and if I needed anything else. My three favorites were all named Rose. Rose, Casinos, and food will be forever linked in my mind.

When the dew was gone, thin flakes like frost on the ground appeared on the desert floor. When the Israelites saw it, they said to each other, "What is it?" For they did not know what it was. Moses said to them, "It is the bread the LORD has given you to eat."

Exodus 16:14-16

Paddle by Moonlight

I knew that it would hot in the South. By the time I reached St. Louis the average temperature was in the mid-90's. Mercifully, the drought had moderated the humidity levels, but it felt hotter than it was. That's called the heat "index" and mid 90's felt well over 100. One night on my marine radio the weather forecaster gave a weather advisory with an anticipated heat index of 109. His advice, "Stay indoors!" So what could I do to beat the heat?

You might assume I could simply jump in the river to cool off. A cynical river-watcher has called the Mississippi a 2000 mile "drainage-ditch". I carefully bathed in the river that one night on the edge of a sand bar. The next day I itched all over, (more on that later). So, why not pour water over your head? Learning from my mistake, I would pour drinking water over my head to cool-off. This brought temporary relief except on days when it was so hot that it felt like a hot, wet towel over my head.

Perhaps the best solution could be summed up in that one magical word: Casinos. As I have mentioned earlier these riverside gambling dens of iniquity were God-sends to me with their sumptuous buffets, air-conditioned comfort, and bathroom sinks (for bathing). But often there were long stretches of river with no casinos. As the heat intensified, it became vital to get off the water in the heat of the day. This became increasingly difficult in the lower river whose banks were levees and shorelines were rocky woods infested with insects and other critters. Some days I simply had to tough it out and keep paddling.

Ultimately I found myself starting my day earlier and earlier. I would pack up my gear using the light of my headlamp and begin my day's journey at dawn. The surrounding scenery may have been prosaic, even ugly, but the sunrises were spectacular. I often slowed to take pictures and savor daybreak. Gradually I found myself rising even earlier and paddling in the predawn light for an hour or more.

One cannot see too many sunrises on the Mississippi.

Mark Twain

I remembered accounts of paddlers journeying on the river at night when they were unable to find a suitable campsite. I would come close to an "all-nighter" south of Baton Rouge when I was chased out of a restricted area by towboats. I began to notice that the rising moon was expanding like a pregnant woman's belly. The Marine Radio Weather predicted a full-moon on July 3. I paddled by its beautiful, piercing bright light for several hours.

This nocturnal solution wasn't without some anxiety. This stretch of river was busy 24/7 with barge traffic. Upriver barges, however, were easy to spot as their blinding searchlights scanned the water ahead. It was a different story with downriver boats which kept my head on a swivel nervously watching for these quiet behemoths surging from behind. Good advice came from a local fisherman, "Listen for the marker buoys, but don't get too close or they will swamp you." I came to recognize the swishing sound in the darkness ahead and to keep it on my starboard side. Often I passed the large green ghosts and could see the water swirling just feet away. As the river had become my teacher, now the darkness taught me lessons. It whispered "Watch and pray!" and "Pray without ceasing". My favorite prayer echoes one attributed to Irish fishermen,

Dear Lord, be good to me.

The sea is so wide,

And my boat is so small.

Paddling in the dark and by moonlight also brought its rewards . In the cool darkness before dawn's early light, as I listened; I heard a solitary bird call out. This voice echoed across the water and soon a reply came and then another. Chirps mingled with caws and cries, twitters joined tweets in a chorus of sound. A symphony surrounded me and life began to skitter and splash all around in the pink and yellow hues fanning across the crystalline surface. The darkness had prepared me to greet the light; anxiety became awe and reticence turned into reverence.

Snake Dance

In the Upper Mississippi animals were my friends. The nearly 500 miles from Lake Itasca to Minneapolis showcases an astonishing variety of wildlife. The river provides home, food supply, and highway for scores of water fowl . Next to Alaska, Minnesota has the greatest number of eagles in the contiguous United States. Watching young eagles learn to fly and hunt was an entertaining prelude to multiple images of majestic, mature, white-capped bald eagles perched high above the water.

Perhaps my favorite bird was the snow-white trumpeter swan. With six foot wingspans, mating pairs could be seen floating amorously in the bogs only to be startled into loud honking flight by our arrival. Raccoons peeking from behind trees, deer swimming across narrow expanses, butterfly flitting between colorful spring flowers, and fuzzy floating flocks of ducklings all provided delightful companionship as we wound our way downstream. The Lower Mississippi River was another story. First it was the "flying fish"!

ASIAN CARP

I can't tell you how many times I was startled by these creatures. Beautiful to behold at a distance, this invasive species known as Asian Carp, would regularly startle me when they would swirl the water next to my boat. You have to understand these are not cute little fish. I would guess that they would average 2-3 feet in length and 10-12 pounds in weight. And they are aggressive. Stimulated by boat motors and by paddle stroke vibrations, they frequently jumped next to, against the side of, and even over my boat. After a 12 hour day of paddling there was nothing more unsettling in the descending dusk as I approached a sand bar in shallow water, than one of these critters leaping out of the water and banging against my kayak.

But these beasts were tame by comparison with two other creatures I was prepared to encounter in the Deep South: Water Moccasins and Alligators. Water moccasins were very dangerous. When I asked a local what I should do if I was bit, he said, "Call 911 and pray!" Living in and along the river I figured I would surely encounter one eventually. I had my own personal "Raiders of the Lost Ark" nightmare where I was surrounded by slithering snakes.

I thought I had come to terms with co-existence until I met Mark as he fished from shore near Osceola, Arkansas. He showed me a video of his stringer of cat fish being snatched from near his feet by a stealthy water moccasin. When asked where moccasins live, he pointed to the rocky rip-rap shoreline levees that I had been regularly stopping by. "They live under the rocks you have been using to get in and out of your boat." From then on I was doubly cautious in my tent at night to check for snakes crawling under my sleeping bag to warm themselves next to my body.

One morning as I broke camp before dawn, I lifted up my ground cloth and out slithered a snake. Illuminated by my head-lap I can only remember screaming like a child and dancing around the snake. I grabbed my paddle and tried to chase the snake away, but it kept crawling under my ground cloth. I have to confess I finally went crazy, hurling epithets and using my paddle to cut the snake into many squiggling pieces.

As I calmed myself, I only hoped that a barge passing in the night hadn't seen my performance. When I finished loading my kayak, I returned to my tent site to check for any supplies I might have forgotten. With the pre-dawn light and my head lamp's beam I discovered that the snake I had filleted couldn't have been more than a foot long. In fact, it was probably a baby!

Later that morning during my prayer time I found myself sounding either very Franciscan or slightly pagan as I prayed for forgiveness for killing this little creature that God had made. Despite this moment of grace, I continued to be hyper vigilant fearing I might encounter a vengeful, slithering relative downstream.

My friend, Jim, had encounters with alligators south of New Orleans, so I kept a watchful eye whenever I approached a "log" along the bank. Locals gave mixed reports. One fellow said that in early July alligator "young' were being born and their large parents were busy catching food for their "congregations". Yes, a group of alligators is called a congregation.

Another group of crusty boat captains told a different tale. Driven from the river by a fierce storm, I met this group in a house near their dock. When I told them of my journey, they warned me, with a twinkle in their eye, about alligators and showed me a video they had shot the week before from their dock. They had hung a chicken on a rope and a 6 foot alligator was leaping out of the water trying to grab a drumstick. Given their salty language and incessant kidding, I took their advice with a grain of salt, but I was happy to be only a day away from the end of my paddle. I was grateful to have completed my journey when I read in the New Orleans Times-Picayune that diving operations on a nearby dock had been suspended because a 12 foot alligator has been seen in the area.

Praise the Lord from the earth, you sea creatures and all deeps.

Psalm 148:7

Peace, be still!

I thought I had seen every imaginable kind of weather by the time I had reached Mississippi. I had survived bone-chilling cold in northern Minnesota. From St. Louis south I had developed ways to deal with the parching drought-driven heat. As I listened faithfully to my marine radio weather forecasts in my tent each night, I now began to hear warnings about "extreme weather" conditions. What could be more extreme than cold and heat? Listening more closely I began to hear new phrases like "a tropical air mass is making its way from the Gulf" and "unstable air where high pressure and low pressure collide". It took words like tornado, gale-force winds, and golf-ball sized hail to get my full attention. Heeding these warnings I began to scan the horizon with great interest to see if the predictions would come true.

Knowing what weather to expect with any certainty was like nailing jello to a wall. Clouds appeared to be drawn to the river like a magnet. Was the river system itself creating its own microclimate and weather? Regularly huge clouds would mass and move quickly across the sky. Sometimes they would be ominous but harmless companions as I paddled. Frequently dark storm clouds would form on one side of the river or downstream and simply pass by like a train heading for another destination. On occasion I was surrounded by foreboding clouds swirling and racing across the skies.

The most alarming aerial displays brought the flashes of lightning followed by surround-sound rumbling thunder. In the early going Jim had warned me about the dangers of lightning. I had thought that I would be safer on the water, but he reminded me that the paddles we were using were made of a composite material that created a perfect lightning rod. He and I had hugged the shore on several occasions in hopes that lightning would target a taller, overhanging tree. In general his advice was if the weather got extreme, get off the water.

The further south I paddled the more extreme the weather forecasts became, and each day I felt like I was dodging storm after storm. One afternoon after lunch at a riverside casino, I saw dark blue-gray clouds forming on the east side of the river. Within minutes they had coalesced into a large funnel shaped cloud which was moving rapidly toward me. I continued paddling in the tail-wind created by the storm front but kept a cautious eye on the front. I hoped this would be just another "false alarm" and that the storm would pass by. Suddenly I heard a roaring sound. A blast of wind like I had never experienced before struck me. Instinctively I paddled for shore, but because the bank was a maze of twisted roots and branches poking out of mud, I couldn't get out of my boat safely. The storm had now completely overtaken me and waves were crashing on the shore. Leaning hard on my rudder and digging deep with a bow stroke I was able to turn my boat into the waves and back into the muddy shore. More accurately the force of the wind and wave now crashing across my bow drove my stern into the bank. Fortunately I was able to grab a branch of a tree and held my prow steady into the cresting waves.

Was this a Tornado? Would it get worse? I hung on for dear life and prayed the storm would pass. Fortunately my spray skirt was secure and the water though turbulent, was relatively warm. To my amazement and relief, after a half-hour of buffeting, the storm passed and the sun came back out. This pattern was repeated numerous times in the coming days. But the most terrifying storm was yet to come.

Before going to sleep I heard that the next day would bring severe weather with thunder and lightning and winds reaching 70 mph. A new wrinkle was added to the weather report. The reporter said that contrary to popular thinking, lightning didn't only hit tall objects like trees. It often traveled though the ground and could electrocute people from below. Great! I could be electrocuted by lightning hitting a nearby tree and carried through the ground to me lying in my tent.

On this particular day the projected time of arrival of this huge storm had been pinpointed to early evening. I made as many miles as I could and began looking for a good, safe place to camp and weather the storm, but the seemingly ever-present sand bars were nowhere in sight. Seeing the storm front on the horizon I chose a moderately high bank and dragged my boat well above the water line, so that if the rain raised the river levels I wouldn't be washed away. The location also had some tall trees nearby for cover but not so near as to fall on my campsite.

After I set up my tent, I dragged several large pieces of driftwood to upwind locations and secured the tent to these logs. I also turned my boat on its side to provide a buffer to the wind. I crawled inside just as the wind began to pick up and the rain started to pelt my rain-fly. Inside my tent I piled all my gear on the upwind side to add ballast in the face of the wind.

With a huge crash of thunder the gale commenced with a force I could never have imagined. Lightning flashed on all sides. As a boy in the Iowa, I remember my grandfather describing a bad storm as a "gully-washer". I hoped I wouldn't be washed away. The wind crescendoed to a deep-throated growl. Its strength pushed against my tent with such force that I feared I would be picked up and thrown into the river. In desperation I stretched out my body and lay prone on the floor of my tent in an attempt to add my body mass to my gear, tent stakes and ropes which were now whistling with the strain of the wind's gusts.

In one of my college classes on spirituality, I teach about various prayer body postures which reflect an attitude of heart. Standing, sitting, and kneeling each would suggest a different spirit. I found I was in the fourth position, prostration, which accurately reflected my helplessness, humility, and submission. A sung prayer that I had often shared on retreats came to mind and became my supplication: "Peace be still, peace be still, the storm rages, peace be still!" Over and over again, I sang and pleaded with God, that the storm might end. My voice was growing hoarse when finally the wind subsided and peace came to my camp. A steady, gentle rain continued lulling me into a grateful sleep.

This day and this night may I know O God

The deep peace of the running wave

The deep peace of the flowing air

The deep peace of the quiet earth

The deep peace of the shining stars

The deep peace of the Son of Peace.

Carmina Gadelica

Redemptive Suffering

Travel journals often focus on highlights, positive events, even mountain-top experiences. This river journey, like life, has had its share of pain. In the early days near the headwaters in northern Minnesota, as I paddled in cold driving rain, I was often tempted to pack it in. This was not fun. I was so cold that I didn't realize I had torn a muscle in my calf and damaged my pinkie causing the nail to eventually fall off.

My hands were so sore it was hard to grip the paddle and impossible to peck out blog updates on my smartphone. A wrist, which I had broken years earlier and stabilized with an inserted plate, throbbed during the night. I lost 15 pounds in the first three weeks. After paddling for 10 hours a day my back ached. Oddly, my arms rarely felt tired or sore. Then there is the mental pain of loneliness and boredom. In sum, it has been a much more difficult and painful experience than I ever imagined.

Certainly suffering and pain can be destructive and debilitating. That is particularly true when it's thrust on us and isn't of our choosing. But it can also make us stronger and more confident when we embrace suffering and let it be our teacher. You know the phrases, *"No gain, no pain!"* or *"The truest steel passes through the fire."* And ultimately, *"There is no Easter without Good Friday."* Suffering becomes redemptive when it leads to "humble boldness."

The Spanish Mystic, St. John of the Cross ((1542-1591) said it this way,

"And I saw a river

over which every soul must pass

to reach the kingdom of heaven

and the name of that river is 'suffering'...

And I saw a boat

which carries souls across the river

and the name of the boat was "love".

The secret of joy is the mastery of pain.

Anais Nin

Dr. King

On my rest day in Memphis I visited the National Civil Rights Museum. Located on the site of the Lorraine Motel where Dr. Martin Luther King Jr. was assassinated in 1968, its displays, pictures, documents, and videos transported me back in time to a very formative period in my life.

I can remember vividly hearing MLK speak at a Luther League (church youth) Convention in Miami Beach in the early 60's. He challenged us to live our faith beyond Sunday into the rest of the week and outside of church onto the streets of our lives. At the time I was living in a small town in Iowa and diversity wasn't about color but about Swedes/Norwegians/ Germans. Over the years Dr. King's writings, speeches, and vision have continued to challenge me. Several other movements (Peace, Women, Environmental) have also shaped my spirituality and life direction. They still do. My river pilgrimage is partly prompted by my deep concern and care for the planet and all creation.

I had forgotten why Dr. King was in Memphis that day. He had come to support the sanitation workers (garbage collectors) whose wages and working conditions were deplorable. The rallying cry of their protests were clear and simple, "I AM A MAN!"

SANITATION WORKER'S STRIKE "I AM A MAN!"

The night before he was shot, Dr. King uttered these still breath-taking words, "I might not be with you, but that does not matter. For I have been to the mountaintop. My eyes have seen the glory!"

I met a bright young Afro-American woman in Memphis. Her name is Kenyarda. She is a special education teacher and has begun work on her Master's degree. In her I see a bit of that "glory"!

Muddy Mississippi

She's called "Old Muddy" and given the fact that the Mississippi River drains 40% of the continental United States, it's a fitting description. The Missouri/Mississippi River system ranks fourth in the world in length

(3,710 miles) following the Nile (4,160 miles), the Amazon (4,000 miles), and the Yangtze Rivers (3,964 miles). Gathering water from the Allegheny Mountains in the east to the Rocky Mountains in the west, it includes all or parts of 31 states and 2 Canadian provinces.

For millennia annual spring floods have scoured topsoil from this region and carried it down stream toward the Gulf of Mexico. Only in this century have these floods been minimized by a system of levees constructed by the Army Corps of Engineers. Snow melt and rainfall continue to scrape the land. As towns have grown into cities and industry has expanded along its banks, the river has become a slurry of soil and chemicals.

At the Lake Itasca headwaters, the water is relatively clear, but it soon turns almost black with the silt it collects winding through marshes, bogs and forests. It's not surprising that wildlife abounds in this more pristine wilderness. Waterfowl are everywhere flying, fishing, and flirting with one another during mating season. Four-legged critters of all sorts wade, wash, and drink streamside. However it isn't long before civilization appears in farms and small towns dot the banks. The sounds of ducks and geese turn to cows mooing as they wade in the water to drink and add their own contributions to the flow. As ever larger bridges begin to cross the river occasional drainage pipes appear carrying runoff. As towns grow larger the pipes grow exponentially in size and carry agricultural, industrial, and human waste. Large red signs start appearing warning boaters to stay clear of large releases of various pollutants.

As I planned for my trip I had wondered if I should bring a water-purifying system so I could use river water for drinking purposes. Soon my reading told me that I should carry my own drinking water. My experience reaffirmed this advice.

After I reached St. Louis and temperatures were often in the high 90's, I thought perhaps that bathing in the river might provide relief. As a boy I remembered swimming in muddy rivers and lakes in Iowa. My inner "Huck Finn" told me to jump in and cool off. One evening after a long day paddling in temperatures over 100 degrees, I set up my tent and waded into the water and lathered up with soap. I felt wonderful as I splashed and rinsed off in the shallows of the sand bar. Instead of lying in my tent and continuing to sweat, I drifted off into a cool, refreshed slumber.

When I awoke the next morning and began to break camp, I began to itch. As the morning progressed I noticed red blotches on my skin and the itching spread to my entire body. The itching turned to stinging as I sweat through the heat of the day. That night I carefully washed my entire body using a couple gallons of my drinking water. I should have remembered that "swimmer's itch" was a regular summer hazard I had experienced as a boy. That was the last time I bathed in Big Muddy.

This lesson was reinforced downriver as I approached Memphis. Paddling near shore to get a better view of the Pyramid shaped sports arena, I narrowly avoided a sudden release of purple effluent spewing from a large industrial complex. I also grew cautious as I approached any kind of loading facility as the air often grew cloudy with colorful dust or pungent vapors. Near Baton Rouge, LA, I encountered another alarming situation. A flotilla of huge barges with enormous cranes was lifting a barge that had sunk with its load of coal to the bottom of the river.

RAISING SUNKEN COAL BARGE

Curious to get a better look, I paddled as close as I dared, only to be sent packing by a loudspeaker warning and an ominous black plume of coal saturated water that began shooting into the air. Despite these toxic experiences folks I met along the river told me, "She's way cleaner than she used to be!" My journey strongly renewed my commitment to stringent environmental laws, like the Clean Water Act of 1972. They are working!

Another abiding environmental impression from the trip occurred as I waited for a lock to open in Iowa. Occasionally I had to wait for a barge to "lock through" and on this day I paddled to a safe place in an upstream backwater. As I rested I slowly surveyed my surroundings. Sitting in my boat I was surrounded by stagnant, brackish water along a rock shoreline littered with plastic bottles and shards of paper and refuse. It felt like sitting in a dirty bathtub. I was embarrassed and saddened that this mess was created by humans.

WAITING IN BACKWATER ABOVE LOCK AND DAM

As I bobbed in the pollution another impression began to emerge as I took a second look at my surroundings. The putrid froth was covered by green algae which seemed to be thriving. Warm rays of sun were working photosynthesis and with it the cleaning of both water and air as well as providing habitat for a variety of life forms. Small fish darted below the surface. Insects buzzed everywhere. Birds flitted in the scraggly brush. And a muskrat clambered over the rocks and slid into the pea-soup. In that moment I was struck by not just the ugliness around me, but also the beauty.

One the one hand our natural environment is fragile, vulnerable, and in great danger due largely to human carelessness. On the other hand, it is amazingly tough and resilient-capable of regeneration and renewal. If there is a lesson to be taken from this experience, it is to stop and pay attention to our natural world. As we do we will be reminded of our responsibility to be good stewards of the garden we have been given to tend and cultivate. The Muddy Mississippi may not be a great place to bathe, but it certainly has helped create a fertile garden on which we can play and from which we can feed the world.

It is not the language of painters but the language of nature which one should listen to ... the feeling for the things themselves, for reality is more important than the feeling for pictures.

Vincent Van Gogh

Pray without ceasing....

From the outset I wanted this journey to be a pilgrimage rather than a trip. I understood a pilgrimage to be a journey to and with God. I remember reading the Canterbury Tales in college as my first exposure to the idea of pilgrimage. Beyond that I knew that a pilgrimage was about being open to whatever happened. It was about not being in control. Each day was a reminder of how out of control I was as I faced weather, river- conditions, and all sorts of critters, including humans, along the way.

I expected that one element I could plan for, however, was prayer. With 12-14 hours of paddling a day I certainly had plenty of time to pray. My prayers were often very spontaneous and weather-related. If I saw a storm coming I immediately prayed that it might pass me by. When it was very cold, my prayers were for warmth and when it was very hot, I asked for a cool breeze. Suffice it to say that my prayers were often very elemental. In fact they came to have a regular, ritualistic, even liturgical formula each day as I traveled through very hot days in the South.

From St. Louis to New Orleans I grew accustomed to baking each day under the sun. Drought conditions made the river levels drop perceptibly each day. As I listened to my marine radio in my tent at night the forecast regularly gave the temperature, heat index, and health advisory. The message was simple, "Stay indoors!" Despite repeated sunscreen applications, my hands had a lizard-skin look. I prayed Psalm 121:

The Lord is my keeper:

the Lord is thy shade upon thy right hand.

The sun shall not smite thee by day,

nor the moon by night.

I soon realized that I needed to get on the water well before sunrise and paddle in the dark to avoid the stifling heat. I would usually paddle from 4 am until just before noon and then attempt to get off the river for a few hours. Even shaded shoreline was oppressively hot, so I often sought refuge in Casinos along the river. But frequently I simply had to paddle through the heat and pray.

My prayer became very specific, "God, I need three things, a 4-6 mph "headwind" to cool me, a strong current to propel me, and a cloud to shade me." Not only was this prayer very specific, but you could set your clock to about 10 am when it would commence and continue uninterrupted for long stretches. I began to understand the biblical admonition "Pray without ceasing...."(I Thessalonians 5:17) with great urgency.

My prayers were not only petitions for weather-relief. Occasionally when they were answered, they were sincere prayers of thanksgiving. If even the slightest breeze rippled the water or a faintest of clouds covered the sun, a "Thank you, Lord!" would flow from deep within.

Lake Providence

Another prayer began south of Memphis. I was told that for several hundred miles there would be virtually no towns along the river to stop for water, supplies, and shelter. Each side of the river was an endless, monotonous levee. Due to drought and low water levels the levees shielded me from seeing what was on the other side, so it felt like paddling through a tunnel. The previous year's flood waters had topped the levees and this perennial threat kept people from building homes along this stretch of the river. Other than passing barges on the river, I was very much alone.

My new prayer was that I would come upon a cabin and people would invite me out of the heat for a cool drink. But mile after mile there were no signs of human habitation. Undaunted, I continued to pray. As time went on I modified my request to simply finding a cabin with a deck and shelter from the sun. That would have been a God-send.

Finally as I paddled through one of the most desolate stretch of river in Northeast Louisiana, I rounded a bend and above a huge sand bar and beyond the levee there appeared to be not one, but three, not just cabins, but houses. I immediately made for shore to see if this was a heat-induced mirage.

I crossed the sand bar and scrambled up the levee to find a large lawn and, yes, three large homes sitting high up on stilts. The one in front of me had a large deck. I didn't care if no one was around. My prayer had been answered and I had found shade from the hot sun.

The sound of machinery distracted my relief and I found a man working on a backhoe under the house. When he saw me, he stopped. After introducing myself, he invited me inside this beautiful air-conditioned home for a cool drink. We were soon joined by two other folks who told me that this compound was the hunting camp for a very rich friend of theirs. They were working on the house to make it less susceptible to flooding. The year before floodwaters had crested the levee and come up to within one foot of the floor.

As we looked out the window of this home I saw my tiny kayak in the distance and figured that the river was at least 60 feet lower this year. As we ate and drank they plied me with questions about my journey down the river and invited me to stay for the night. Needing to make miles on the river, I declined their gracious invitation, but enjoyed several hours of rest and refreshment.

RICHARD, KYLE, AND GUY AT LAKE PROVIDENCE, LA.

As I headed back to my boat, Richard said he would see me off. Just before I pushed off, he said "Wait a minute..." And he took my hands and asked if he could pray for me. As he prayed for my safe passage down the river, I had tears in my eyes. Once again God had answered my prayer far beyond what I could have ever imagined. Later that night in my tent when I looked at my maps to trace the day's course, I found my midday stop had been at Lake Providence.

Barge Bullies

In the early going my little boat felt way too big for the river. With banks close together, tree limbs and snags, shallow water, and incessant twists and turns, simply making forward progress was a challenge. But as the river grew in size, I began to feel much smaller. Head winds would buffet and slow me to a crawl. Dams would stop me altogether and require leaving the water to unload the kayak and drag it for long distances in a portage before re-launching.

From Minneapolis south a series of dams and locks required getting permission to enter, lock through, and exit below in usually boiling water. Often I was the only boat in the lock as the water slowly lowered. From time to time a larger pleasure craft would provide company. But never the big boats...the barges.

I had heard stories about these large vessels and the basic message was "stay clear". It's hard to anticipate just how large barges are until one would come around a bend in the river and soon occupy my entire field of vision. You see, barges aren't a single boat but a powerful "towboat" powered by jet engines pushing multiple, huge containers filled with a variety of goods ranging from coal to rock to chemicals. The largest assembly I encountered numbered 36 separate containers and seemed to take forever to pass by as I got out of the way.

The greatest danger was the huge wake thrown up by the tow boat. Four to five foot surges of water were common and often the entire river would be a swirling mass of whirlpools and eddies for a mile downriver after a barge passed. Each day my frequently repeated ritual was to give a wide birth and a respectful wave as my big barge brothers lumbered by. If the captain saw me I would receive a wave and a loud blast on the ship's horn.

For the most part barges were my friends. That all changed south of Baton Rouge, LA. The river was at an all-time low due to drought conditions and safe passage became more hazardous within narrowing shorelines. This was also the stretch of the river that is actually a part of the "harbor" stretching from New Orleans over 100 miles upriver to a bridge that is impassable for ocean-going vessels. Bigger ships ... smaller river!

I had just left the cool and tasty confines of the Belle of Baton Rouge Casino. After a midday break from the heat I hoped to paddle a few hours before camping at sunset. A sudden rain squall drove me off the river for shelter. When I got back on the river its banks were lined with barges awaiting favorable upriver travel conditions.

I had donned my reflective vest so that my little boat might be seen among the "big boys". As the light diminished I strapped on my head lamp to increase my visibility. I kept watching for the usually frequent sand-bars that had become my camping sites for several weeks. But none were to be seen. The river traffic was high and as sunset approached towboats seemed to be everywhere moving individual barges into large configurations in preparation for transport. As I hugged the shore the smell of chemicals singed my nostrils. By now I knew the smell of Benzene from having passed flotillas of this toxic chemical with huge red signs warning boats to "STAY AWAY".

I had no choice but to continue paddling in search of a camp-site. Dusk had turned to dark and anxiousness had turned to near panic. I wondered if my little bobber of a boat was visible to anyone.

I suddenly had an answer as I was blinded by a piercing light. Shading my eyes I saw a Towboat ahead with its spotlight trained on me. A loud speaker began blaring, "You are trespassing......" Before I knew it several other spotlights hit me. Multiple voices were shouting epithets. The water around me began to boil. The towboat had been joined by several others and I was surrounded like a kid on the playground by a group of barge bullies taunting me.

Fear mixed with rage as I realized my plight and screamed out over the din, "Leave me alone.... I am looking for a place to camp. Do you know where there's a sand bar?" The boats slowly backed off and I heard a voice shouting, "Downriver, port.....get out of here NOW!" I needed no further persuading as I stroked hard and fast fleeing these barge bullies. My problem wasn't solved, however.

It was now dark. Paddling in the dark was not new, as I had for weeks gotten up before dawn to avoid the heat and headed out on the water. But now river traffic was everywhere, the wind was picking up, and no sandbar was on the horizon. I wondered if "Downriver, port!" was simply a taunt or even bad information. I knew I could paddle through the night, but I was tired and, frankly, scared.

After about an hour I saw a cluster of lights on the opposite shore of the river. It looked like one of the many oil refineries I had passed as commerce now lined the shores. The lights seemed to illumine what looked like a sand bar. Was this my safe haven? The head-wind was now throwing up waves across the bow of my boat and the spray blurred my vision. Sandy beach? Mirage?

To find out I would have to cross the river which was now a mile wide. Crossing the river wasn't a problem, but crossing the channel at night amid huge barges and tankers was a new and frightening prospect. Scanning the river and seeing no ships I decided to go for it! Paddling with a steady and forceful stroke I headed toward the distant lights. The breaker's drum beat was punctuated by my staccato strokes as I crossed the channel. I searched ahead for the sight of a red marker buoy which would signal the far side of the channel and relative safety. I didn't dare stop to clean my glasses. As I reached mid-channel I heard a thunderous sound above the howling wind. It was the blaring horn of a barge.

I didn't need to look to know that I was in its path as it surged downstream.

BARGES EMERGING FROM THE FOG

I also knew instinctively that if I did look back to get my bearings and the barge's position relative to mine, it might be the last thing I saw on this earth. Adrenaline coursed through my body as my stroke became a blur of paddle, water, and dread. One image flashed across my mind, surfing down

8 foot waves on Big Winnie. As the image faded another appeared just as quickly. It was a red buoy bobbing wildly in the frothy chop. In that instant I knew I would make it and looked back behind me as the barge roared past.

As I relaxed my stroke and glided into the sand bar I whispered what was becoming my regular prayer , "Oh God, thy sea is so great, and my boat is so small!" This story would not be shared in my blog. It would have to wait until I was safe and at home!

CLOSE TO HOME

The Communion of Saints and the Dead Poet's Society

Do you ever talk to dead people? Come on...be honest! I do. A few years after my dad died, I found myself occasionally having conversations with him. I might ask a question or wonder aloud with him about a problem seeking his advice. Usually I reflected on what a great dad he was and would simply thank him. And I believe he is listening. I know that I am not alone in this practice because when I have asked others they readily admit to talking to a parent, grandparent, close friend, or teacher.

Recently on my Mississippi River paddle I had lots of time on my hands. I found myself talking regularly with my dad. But it didn't stop there. Passing under magnificent cloud formations I thought of the bible passage in the letter to the Hebrews which uses the image of being surrounded by a "cloud of witnesses" to describe those people who, though dead, are present with us. Being an athlete I imagined this cloud as bleachers filled with supporters cheering me on in my life-journey. As I endured bone-numbing, wind-driven rain or withering 100 degree heat and humidity, I was encouraged to know that I wasn't alone....my dad and others were cheering me on. But one day I began to see other faces in the clouds of witnesses. There were family members, former teachers and mentors, even historical figures. This was really getting interesting.

DICK AND LEILA ELLINGSON: NEWLYWEDS

Then I remembered the phrase in the Apostle's Creed, the basic summary of what Christians believe.

"I believe in the communion of saints..." Might that "communion of saints" be the "cloud of witnesses" cheering me from the packed bleachers? As I came to this conclusion I wondered why I had never heard this described or discussed in church. We do talk about "saints" at least once a year on All Saints Day. Maybe speaking with or praying to the saints is too "catholic" for Lutherans.

Classmate, friend, and colleague, Dr. Timothy Lull, was a world-renowned Luther scholar. Tim once told me that he was so immersed in the life of Martin Luther that he often felt Luther's presence in his study as he prepared to teach his classes. Ultimately this led Dr. Lull to write a delightful little book called <u>My Conversations with Martin Luther</u>. If such a highly respected professor as Timothy Lull spoke regularly with Martin Luther, maybe I wasn't crazy after all.

Back to the river...as I thought more and more about those witnesses who had shaped my life and faith the list grew...the bleachers became a cheering stadium. As I paddled under the river clouds I set aside time to imagine the "cloud of witnesses". Sometimes I spoke with an individual and engaged him or her in lively conversation. Often I offered a prayer of thanks for helping me on my journey. Regularly I panned the entire cloud-crowd and visualized them bathed in light.

Are you still with me? What do you think? Am I crazy? Or have we lost sight of a wonderful resource for our lives in the "cloud of witnesses" and "communion of saints"?

A favorite movie of mine is the Dead Poet's Society. In it, Mr. Keating, an English teacher, played by Robin Williams, encouraged his students to live boldly.

One day he took his class to look at the school trophy case to see the pictures of the school's past heroes. "Lean in and listen to what they are saying......" he tells them.....as he whispers loudly "Carpe Diem" "Carpe Diem" "Carpe Diem" which means "seize the day". A small group of students took his advice and revived the Dead Poet's Society which met regularly in a cave to read poetry aloud and listen to wisdom of "dead poets".

As followers of Jesus we have our own "dead poet's society" populated by generations of "heroes of the faith". These saints played an important role in helping me paddle 2350 miles down the Mississippi River. Who are those heroes and saints in your life? Take some time by yourself. Be quiet and listen carefully. What are they saying? I suspect that they are cheering you on!

"Carpe Diem!"

Stand by Me

I have to confess that the lower Mississippi is a rather ugly stretch. The water is pretty rank after 2000 miles draining 40% of the continent. Big Muddy has become a toxic highway of chemicals and waste materials, with the shoreline an endless succession of refineries, container docks, power plants and grain elevators. The pristine beauty of the headwaters was a distant memory. Even the majestic green limestone bluffs which frame the river in Iowa and Wisconsin were all but forgotten.

Now the river felt like an obstacle course as I dodged barges and ships that belonged on the ocean. As I approached Baton Rouge I was also doing my best to not get caught in a sudden and violent storm which could suddenly sweep across the river with fierce lightning bolts and kayak-shaking thunder claps. I was in the home-stretch with only a few hundred miles to paddle. I could almost taste New Orleans. But first I had to survive this gauntlet of danger.

One evening as I paddled between riprap-lined banks doing my best to steer clear of one of the many dangers, I realized there were no more sand bars to conveniently plop down my tent. Coach Lewis had warned me that in this part of the river "you will probably sleep in a vertical position and not very well…" As the shadows lengthened I began to worry that his prediction would come true. Wearily I paddled mile after mile with no camp spots anywhere to be seen.

Just before the sun went down I spied some folks fishing across the river. I figured that if they could get to the bank, perhaps a camping spot was nearby or they could tell me where to find one. Once again I raced across the channel pointing my boat upstream from their location so that my hard strokes and the river's steady current would land me at their feet.

As I approached I saw three young boys fishing by their four-wheelers. By now I was accustomed to the quizzical looks of folks to this strange-looking person in a tiny red kayak. I asked how the fishing was going and if there were places I might camp. They pointed me to a little patch of mud. As I disembarked they cheerfully dragged the Leila V II up on the bank. Sitting by my craft they introduced themselves as Hunter, Wayne, and Nick.

WAYNE, HUNTER, AND NICK SOUTH OF BATON ROUGE, LA

Eager to hear about my adventure, they plied me with questions about food, weather, and animals along the way. Suddenly Hunter asked, "Are you hungry or thirsty?" Without pause, I blurted, "Always…." Telling me that they lived nearby, they jumped on their 4 wheelers and motored off to get some grub to feed their new friend.

By the time they returned I had precariously set up my tent on my new mud-home and was ready for whatever they had found when they raided their home kitchen. The menu included two chilled Cokes and a Capri Sun to wash down three cans of Chef Boyardee Meatballs and Spaghetti. As I gulped down the cokes, I hid my vegetarian ways by saying I would save the Chef until tomorrow.

As the sun went down the boys shared a bit of their journeys and their dreams of becoming a welder, a mechanic, and a heavy equipment operator. It was dark when they departed with my thanks and good wishes that their dreams would come true. As I lay in my tent a song came to mind,

When the night has come and the land is dark

And the moon is the only light we see

No, I won't be afraid, oh, I won't be afraid

Just as long as you stand, stand by me.

If the sky that we look upon should tumble and fall

Or the mountain should crumble into the sea

I won't cry, I won't cry, no, I won't be afraid

Just as long as you stand, stand by me.

As this great Ben E. King song played in my mind, I went to sleep with a prayer of thanks for Hunter, Wayne, and Nick, my "Stand by Me" boys.

Recalling this experience a couple months later I realized that this song may have been inspired by a favorite scripture, Psalm 46:2

Therefore, we will not fear though the earth gives way

And the mountains fall into the midst of the sea!

All that Jazz

As I neared the end of my journey my focus was downriver. While carefully avoiding danger posed by huge ocean-going ships, I pushed forward on "auto-pilot" with the river bank's industry only a peripheral blur. Beyond the levees an occasional sign would appear signaling population centers and a succession of towns leading to New Orleans.

It was mid-morning and getting hot as I spotted out of the corner of my eye an I-HOP sign. Unfortunately the current was strong and the river traffic heavy and I had passed this attractive pit-stop before I could safely head to shore. Determined to not make that mistake again I began scouring the horizon for eateries. Nothing...

What ultimately caught my eye was a large cross on a church steeple. Close by was a rare ferry-landing and an even rarer beach where I hurriedly landed the *Leila V. II* The passengers in the cars awaiting passage presented the usual looks of disbelief as I clambered by in my bright orange shirt, shorts, floppy river-hat and paddle in hand.

Cresting the grass-covered dike I immediately saw the edifice of a large Catholic church whose cross and steeple had called me from the river. Alongside the church was one of the unique cemeteries the area is known for. Because this area of the delta is well below the level of the river and protected by tall earthen levees, the high water table requires graves be above-ground. It looked like a little city of small houses for the dead.

Crossing a busy highway hoping to find a place to eat, I spied a number of ancient "shot-gun" houses, known for the long and narrow shape which would allow the discharge of a gun to pass from the front to the back door. In front of one of the houses was a small blackboard with the scribbled inscription, "Lunch 11-3". As I opened the door the wail of a trumpet and the smell of Southern hospitality welcomed me. Looking around, the walls were covered with old black and white pictures. The largest picture was of the legendary Louis "Satchmo" Armstrong. Pictures of a variety of jazz greats gave the place the feel of a shrine or a museum. Behind the counter was a handsome, elderly black gentleman. On the wall next to the cash register was a framed newspaper article featuring famous jazz percussionist and composer, Eddie "Duke" Edwards, looking much like a dapper, young Denzel Washington. Glancing from the picture to the man taking my order, I immediately saw that I was talking to Eddie.

EDDIE "DUKE" EDWARDS, EDWALL, LA.

Having just come from cooking in the kitchen, he wiped the sweat from his brow and dished up a plate full of red beans and rice, green beans, and macaroni and cheese. Business was slow, so when I told him I was paddling down the river, he asked if he could join me and learn more about my trip.

For the next hour we swapped tales. He was impressed by my adventure almost as much as I was of his stories of playing with Satchmo and Charlie "Bird" Parker, touring the world, and writing scores for Hollywood movies. Eddie, now 78 years old, had returned to his Edwall, LA home to be near his 3 children and 18 grandchildren. He had recently opened this little restaurant called the Creole Quickstop to serve up some good home-cookin and provide a venue for some quality jazz.

As we chatted, his daughter, Desiree, came in and joined the conversation. A singer and actress she told me of her most recent "gig" in the Quentin Tarentino movie, *Django Unchained*, which was shot on a nearby plantation. The Quickstop had been a favorite place for the crew to hang out!

Once again I was blown away by an amazing "chance encounter". By now I was convinced that "chance" had nothing do with another pair of "river angels" joining me on my paddle down the Mississippi.

This wasn't my last visit to the Quickstop. After finishing my trip, I had a few hours to kill before catching my plane back home to Seattle. Checking the map I found that the restaurant was near the airport, so a friend and I had a return engagement with Eddie and Desiree! Sitting on the porch we savored the best Southern cooking accompanied by the soothing sounds of Satchmo! It doesn't get any better, not even at I-HOP!

You're in the army now!

What would a good ending to my journey look like? I had plenty of time to imagine and plan! For two and a half months I had been paddling an average of 12 hours a day. In downtown New Orleans near the Cathedral square there are a series of steps down to the river. I had many times sat on those steps and watched the ferry going back and forth across the busy river. This popular spot on the River Walk seemed like the perfect place to disembark. But a problem had emerged during my descent of the Lower Mississippi. Drought conditions had lowered the river to near record levels. While this had provided me with regular sandbar accommodations for pitching my tent each night, it meant that those steps would now be a high and unscaleable wall. I needed a "Plan B".

Through a local friend I learned of and sought the advice of a retired Coast Guard official. He would certainly know a good place to exit the river. We chatted via cell phone and he suggested Audubon Park. Its accessible levee would make pulling my kayak out of the water relatively easy. That was the plan. But as was often the case, the best laid plans.......

The day started well as I eagerly broke camp for my final day on the river and my hoped-for triumphal entry into Big Easy. By now dodging massive ocean-going ships seemed routine. The huge wakes thrown at me were like a fun amusement park ride. It appeared that everyone I saw on barges and ships waved a greeting as they recognized my accomplishment.

Almost hypnotized by a parade-like atmosphere, I didn't notice the sudden change in the weather. Fortunately, a fellow on a dock waved his arms as I approached and pointed behind me. Looking back I saw a wall of black clouds coming downriver. Dockside he said, "You better get off the river....that's a bad one!" Directing me around to a rock and mud bank behind the dock, I dragged my boat on-shore just as the storm hit. I secured the Leila V II and stumbled through a tangle of brush as I was pelted with rain and blasted by gusts of wind.

My new friend met me and opened the door to a small dockside building. Inside I stood dripping on the floor of a headquarters of a boat provisioning company. Gathered around a table and watching TV was a motley collection of captains of several of the boats docked outside in the driving rain. They welcomed me as I began to shed my wet gear and hung it up to dry. For the next three hours as the storm raged outside I got to know this amazing bunch of guys.

The stereotype of a foul-mouthed bunch of sailors fit this group perfectly as the blue-language flew around. It felt like I had come onboard a ship from Pirates of the Caribbean. But the group was equally generous and kind as they invited me to help myself to anything I wanted in their well-stocked kitchen.

For several hours we swapped tales of my adventure and their life tending the big ships. These were the guys who had teased a 6 foot alligator with the "chicken on a string" They took special pleasure in showing me a video they had shot of their caper right out front where I had exited the river. They also warned me that the woods I had passed through to get to their building was home to a family of water moccasins. As the rain subsided they told me I had a window of a few hours before the next storm front, so I better get going. Off I went!

River traffic began to pick up as I passed under the Huey Long Bridge. A towboat pilot I had seen before near Baton Rouge waved and shouted congratulations as I entered a stretch of river with both banks lined by barges. The skyline of NOLA was now in view as I began scanning the shoreline for my takeout spot at Audubon Park. As the bank of barges ended I spied a tree-lined shore and large grassy areas. This must be it, I thought. Even better there was a concrete ramp to drag my boat out of the water. I had made it.

The day was now hot and sunny; perfect conditions for laying out all my wet gear to dry. I called a friend I would be staying with to come and pick me and the boat up. Despite the heat I savored the feeling of accomplishment. As my gear dried I walked up to the top of the ramp and onto a large grassy area next to several modern multi-storied buildings. Coming upon what looked like a helicopter landing pad I called my friend with more exact directions to my location. Next to the pad was a flagpole with a large familiar flag flying.

I had seen this flag often on my trip down the river. Against a red background was a brown castle turret and below it the inscription of the Army Corps of Engineers. That should have been my first clue. But I headed back down the ramp and packed up all my gear and got it ready for pickup. By now my friend should have arrived, I thought.

As I walked back up the ramp and across the helipad, I saw a large fence and a guard booth. As I crested the hill a fully uniformed soldier came running my way with a gun in hand. He was shouting, "What are you doing here? You are on a military base. This is private property."

I expected that he would understand and even be impressed when I told him I had just paddled down the entire Mississippi River. He wasn't impressed. He gruffly shouted, "This is a military base. Put your boat back in the water and leave immediately!"

I am not sure what motivated my response. I suspect it was a mixture of exhaustion and naiveté. But I simply said, "I just unpacked my boat. I am hot and tired. I am not going back on the river. My friend is coming to pick me up." I tried to be courteous, but he wasn't having any of it. He repeated his message. I added, "I would like to speak with your superior!" I figured that if this tactic worked to get my cellphone bill corrected, it would work now. As I waited outside the guard station I called my wife on my cellphone to let her know that I had arrived safely in NOLA. When the guard returned I told my wife "I gotta go!"

Once again the guard repeated his now familiar refrain. Frustrated at this disheveled looking river-rat disobeying his orders, I could now see he was getting angry. But so was I. So I said, "Throw me in the brig!" What did I just say, I thought? But then a night in jail and a good meal might be an improvement over my recent accommodations. This was getting a bit crazy.

I could now see my friend's car arriving at the gate. Coming from the other direction was the commanding officer. As the crowd grew I explained my situation to the commanding officer. Probably to avoid the situation escalating and as a way of washing his hands and passing the buck, he called the local NOLA police and said it was "their issue". When they arrived we all rehearsed our well-worn lines, but with a very different result.

When the local cop heard my story, he asked, "You really paddled down the whole river......?" I could see on the guard's face a look of disappointment. I think he would have been happy to throw me in the brig. To be fair, he was just doing his duty. The local cops quickly surveyed the scene and with the approval of the commanding officer, said, "Get your boat loaded and move out!" As we loaded the boat the cops helped and peppered me with questions about my paddling adventure. As we pulled out the gate, I tried to tell the guard that I didn't mean any trouble. He frowned and waved me off!

Later that night when I called my wife to tell her the rest of the story, she interrupted me and said, "I heard the whole thing....your phone was on the whole time." I have a hunch that she would have sided with the guard. Like many of my river experiences, this day didn't go as planned. But "Plan C" is a much better story!

New Orleans

EPILOGUE

I always loved the word "penultimate" which is a fancy way of saying these are "final" thoughts or reflections, but not really.......there may be more to come. This seems particularly fitting when speaking of a pilgrimage because it never ends. Like a river there is always something or someone around the next bend. And even as the river flows into the sea, or in my case the Gulf of Mexico, there is now an ocean of paddling ahead. One more pen-penultimate thought: Many of you who followed my blog down the river asked if I was planning to write a book.

Initially I thought I wouldn't, because I am finishing another book that I began early in my sabbatical. I thought the blog would tell the story with more immediacy and, frankly, would be easier to accomplish "in real time". A blog would also help me keep track of the blurring of days and experiences on the river.

Since I have returned home to Seattle, I have found my mind continuing to remember "stories" which I didn't tell in the blog. But would anyone other than my 96 year old mother, Leila V., be interested? So I tested out some of the stories with friends here and they encouraged me to write them down. This book answers the question. It is also dedicated to my mom, who survived my trip, but who passed away on April 8, 2013, just a few months short of her 97th birthday. As you know my two boats were named after her and it is with great love and gratitude that I dedicate this book to her.

Whether spoken or communicated by "raised-eyebrow" or "rolling eyes", you asked, "why?' I am glad you did. It helped me to create a frame from which to imagine and plan my paddle pilgrimage. That preflection helped me to discover what had lead me to embark on this epic journey with great enthusiasm . Now that the actual paddle is completed, my "reflection" helps me make sense of all the amazing people, places, and experiences along the way with even greater gratitude. I celebrate the "why" and encourage you to embark on the adventures you have been preparing a lifetime for and which will change your life forever.

Adventure:

As a boy growing up near the Mississippi River I was fascinated by this little stream that I could walk across at its headwaters but I could barely see across at its widest expanse. My turtle friend, Minn, (*Minn of the*

Mississippi by H.C. Holling) was my guide down the river introducing me to the sounds, sights, smells, and feel of this watery world. The "Huck Finn" in me delighted in the variety of characters I met along the banks of the Mighty Mississippi. They became river angels who provided food, housing, transportation, encouragement, and a multitude of stories. Big cities (Minneapolis, St. Louis, Memphis) and small towns (Osceola, St. Francisville, New Madrid) came to life and became neighborhoods populated by family and friends.

Learn:

As a professor on sabbatical, my river journey focused on "Creation Care: Environmental Ethics". Studying history I learned that the Anishinabe people (Ojibwe Indian) called the river "Mee-zee-see-bee" which means "Big River" or "Father of Waters". The wisdom of their name became apparent as I encountered the birds (326 species) and fish (241 species) who now uneasily share their polluted home with thousands of boats, barges and ships which ply the waters transporting grain, coal, and hazardous cargo (oil, benzene). Keeping the water clean for fish and fowl and clear for barges and business requires a delicate balance much like a kayaker carefully navigating the human debris flowing inexorably to the sea.

JIM AND SHARRON LEWIS IN GRAND RAPIDS, MN.

NATHAN, LORI, TODD AND SAM IN MINNEAPOLIS, MN.

Pilgrimage:

As a pilgrim my journey was in search of the One who created this garden planet and whose "heavens declare the glory of God" (Psalm 19:1) With few distractions and lots of time to listen and pay attention, God used the river to teach me both how powerful and regenerative the natural environment is but also how fragile and in need of wise care and stewardship it is. My kinship with all creation now resonates more deeply with St. Francis' "brother Sun and sister Moon". Each morning just before dawn a symphony of birds began their musical wake-up call and invited me to launch my boat in the dark and paddle toward the light. They called me to a new day, to a new beginning, a new life, and to pray. Thanks be to the God revealed by Mother Earth and the Father of Waters!

Finally, thanks to all who followed my journey and supported me with your prayers, words of encouragement, and even your occasional, "You're doing what???"

Blessings to each of you on your "pilgrimage"!

Dave

Tell me, what is it you plan to do with your one wild and precious life?

Mary Oliver

Appendix
Resources/Websites:

www.nrpe.org The National Religious Partnership for the Environment

www.greenfaith.org Inspiring, educating, and mobilizing people from diverse religious backgrounds for environmental leadership

www.earthministry.org Resources for churches and their environmental ministries.

www.lutheransrestoringcreation.org Religious Enviromental Education Resources

www.waymarkers.net Resources on Pilgrimage and Celtic Spirituality

www.progressivechristianity.org Programs/resources inspired by theologian/author, Matthew Fox

www.earthandspiritcenter.org Programs/resources inspired by cosmologist/author, Thomas Berry

www.cedartreeinstitute.org Leadership for collaborative efforts in mental health, religion, and the environment.

www.bucktrack.com Books and advice from adventurer Buck Nelson.

Made in the USA
Charleston, SC
10 September 2014